I N T E R N E T

BROWSING
THE WEB

ABOUT THIS BOOK

Browsing The Web is an easy-to-follow guide to Microsoft's Web-browsing program, Internet Explorer. This book is for people with very little experience of using Internet Explorer.

INTERNET EXPLORER'S ESSENTIAL features, from launching the program to personalizing Internet Explorer, are presented in separate chapters to allow easy understanding of their functions.

Within each chapter, you'll find subsections that also deal with self-contained procedures. Each of these procedures builds on the knowledge that you will have accumulated by reading the previous chapters.

The chapters and the subsections use a step-by-step approach. Almost every step is accompanied by an illustration showing how your screen should look. The screen images are either full-screen or they focus on an important detail that you'll see on your own screen. If you work through the steps, you'll soon start feeling comfortable that you're learning and making progress.

The book contains several features to help you understand what is happening and what you need to do. A labeled Internet

Explorer window is included to show you where to find the important elements in Internet Explorer. This is followed by an illustration of the rows of buttons, or "toolbars," at the top of the screen, to help you find your way around these invaluable, but initially perplexing, controls.

The command keys that you use, such as ENTER and BACKSPACE, are shown in these rectangles: Enter ← and ← Bksp, so that there is no confusion, for example, over whether you should press that key, or type the letters "bksp." Cross-references are shown within the text as left- or right-hand page icons: and . The page number within the icon and the reference are shown at the foot of the page.

As well as the step-by-step sections, there are boxes that explain a feature in detail, and tip boxes that provide alternative methods and shortcuts. Finally, at the back, you will find a glossary explaining new terms and a comprehensive index.

ESSENTIAL DK COMPUTERS

INTERNET

BROWSING
THE WEB

ANNALISA MILNER

A Dorling Kindersley Book

Dorling Kindersley
LONDON, NEW YORK, DELHI, SYDNEY

Produced for Dorling Kindersley Limited by
Design Revolution, Queens Park Villa,
30 West Drive, Brighton, East Sussex BN2 2GE

EDITORIAL DIRECTOR Ian Whitelaw
SENIOR DESIGNER Andy Ashdown
EDITOR John Watson
DESIGNER Andrew Easton

MANAGING EDITOR Sharon Lucas
SENIOR MANAGING ART EDITOR Derek Coombes
DTP DESIGNER Sonia Charbonnier
PRODUCTION CONTROLLER Wendy Penn

First American Edition, 2000

2 4 6 8 10 9 7 5 3 1

Published in the United States by Dorling Kindersley, Inc.
95 Madison Avenue, New York, New York, 10016

Published in Great Britain by Dorling Kindersley.

A catalog record is available from the Library of Congress.

ISBN 0-7894-5527-7

Color reproduced by First Impressions, London
Printed in Italy by Graphicom

For our complete
catalog visit
www.dk.com

CONTENTS

THE WORLD WIDE WEB

The World Wide Web, commonly known as "the Web," is the largest and fastest growing area of the Internet. This chapter tells you how it works and what you can do on the Web.

WHAT IS THE WEB?

The World Wide Web is a vast information resource that exists around the world on hundreds of thousands of computers called Web servers. These contain websites that can vary in content from a single page to many thousands of pages that are electronically linked to each other. The total number of pages now available on the World Wide Web is numbered in billions. These pages add up to a global library of information that you can access and navigate by using your computer.

HOW THE WEB WORKS

The World Wide Web consists of countless pages all connected via the global communications network provided by the Internet. The connections are made by hypertext links, or "hyperlinks," which are addresses embedded in the Web pages. These links may connect to pages on the same website, or to a computer on the other side of the planet.

Your PC
You access the Web from your PC via a modem and an Internet Service Provider.

Web browser
You request Web pages from Web servers by typing a unique address into a program called a Web browser.

Modem
Modems enable computers to communicate with each other over the telephone network.

HOW DO YOU ACCESS THE WEB?

To access the Web you need a personal computer connected to a modem – an electronic device that translates the computer's digital signals into the analog signals that can pass along telephone lines. You also need an account with an Internet Service Provider (ISP), which operates powerful computers permanently connected to the Internet, and is your gateway to the Web. Through your modem and your ISP, you can explore what is available on the Web by using a program called a Web browser.

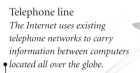

Telephone line
The Internet uses existing telephone networks to carry information between computers located all over the globe.

Satellite
Satellites can form part of the Internet network.

Service provider
Your ISP translates the Web address and sends your request to the correct Web server on the Internet.

Web server
A Web server is a large computer that stores Web pages and makes them available over the Internet. It receives your request and sends the data for the relevant Web page back to your PC.

ISN'T THE WEB THE SAME AS THE INTERNET?

Many people use the terms "World Wide Web" and "Internet" to mean the same thing, but they are different. The Internet is a global network of interconnected computers that communicate with each other via the existing telecommunications networks. The Web uses the Internet network to access and link websites. As well as providing the infrastructure over which the World Wide Web is able to operate, the Internet offers a variety of other forms of communications and resources, including email, newsgroups, and discussion groups. If the Internet is like a system of roads linking places together, then requests for Web pages, and the data from Web pages, are just two of the many kinds of traffic that travel on this road system.

WHAT'S ON THE WEB?

The pages of the World Wide Web offer information on just about every topic you care to think of. Whether your interests include current affairs, astrophysics, golf, or Antarctic flora and fauna, somewhere there is certain to be a website devoted to that topic. The Web has always been the home of academic information, but in recent years it has also become an information base for public sector bodies, government departments and, most noticeably, commercial organizations.

Nonprofit organizations
Most major charities and non-profit organizations promote their work on the Web.

News
Broadcast corporations provide up-to-the-minute news of global events on the Web, often before it goes out over the airwaves.

Education
Many leading universities and independent bodies offer courses that can be studied over the Web.

Online games
You can pit your wits against opponents all round the world with online games.

Commercial organizations
You can buy anything over the Web, from books and clothes to your weekly groceries.

Research
Libraries, universities, public and commercial bodies, and individuals all publish information on the Web.

Government bodies
To email the President or contact your local council, you will almost certainly find the right address on a website.

Hobbyists
Individuals create their own websites on topics they are interested in, but amateur information is not always reliable.

WHAT'S ON A WEB PAGE?

When the Web started, Web pages contained only text and very basic formatting, and they offered very little in the way of design. Today's Web pages are a world away from those early pioneers and many sites now aspire to be multimedia extravaganzas. A Web page is likely to incorporate sophisticated graphics and include video clips, sound sequences, and interactive animations. You may even be able to play miniature software programs knows as "applets" on the page.

Download files
Web pages can contain files that you transfer to your own computer to view or install.

Programs
While you are viewing a site, a program can run independently within the Web page.

Graphics
A well-designed website can be a showcase for the skills of the graphic designer.

Hypertext links
Use hypertext links, or "hyperlinks," to go directly to other relevant sites.

Text
Text within a page can be copied, pasted, and saved to your hard disk.

Multimedia files
These can be sound, video, or interactive animations.

Photographs
Images on a Web page can also act as hyperlinks.

25 **Recognizing hypertext links**

WHAT IS A WEB BROWSER?

A Web browser is a piece of software installed on your PC that lets you look at (or "browse") different websites. The most widely used Web browsers are Netscape Navigator and Microsoft Internet Explorer. Navigator was the first to arrive and quickly became the most popular browser on the market. Microsoft then created its own browser, called Internet Explorer, and ever since there has been a strong rivalry between the two, but both are excellent browsers. You can have both of them installed on your PC, and which one you use is a matter of personal preference.

WHICH PROGRAM?

The examples shown in this book use Internet Explorer, but the pages should look almost the same using Netscape Navigator. New versions of these browsers are released from time to time. For example, Internet Explorer 5 replaced version 4, adding new features. It is best to use the most recent release of either browser providing your PC has sufficient memory and speed to support it.

Netscape Navigator
Has a similar toolbar to Internet Explorer.

Internet Explorer
The pages look almost the same as Netscape Navigator.

MORE ABOUT BROWSERS

Most websites look the same regardless of which browser you use. But you might notice small changes if you use both. This is because HTML (the programming language for Web pages, called the Hypertext Markup Language) describes how a page appears, and different browsers may interpret these instructions differently. Also, Netscape Navigator and Internet Explorer support some tags that are unofficial features of HTML designed to give users a reason to use that particular browser. But these features are not widely used – most websites stick to using "official" HTML, so that all browsers can read the page correctly.

UNDERSTANDING WEB ADDRESSES

Web addresses are known as URLs. This stands for Universal (sometimes Uniform) Resource Locator. URLs are made up of two distinct parts: a protocol and a domain name. The protocol, the first part of the URL, tells the Web browser what type of site it is contacting – a website, a file transfer site, or a secure website, for example. In this case the protocol is http, standing for Hypertext Transfer Protocol, the standard for Web communications. The second part, the domain name, is like a street address – it tells the Web browser where to go to find the site.

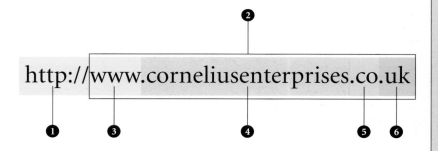

THE DIFFERENT PARTS OF A WEB ADDRESS

1 Protocol
Most Web addresses begin with http://. This stands for Hypertext Transmission Protocol. This protocol is used to transfer ordinary Web pages over the Internet. Other protocols you are likely to encounter are ftp:// (file transfer protocol) and https://. This protocol is used on "secure" websites, for sending and receiving sensitive information.

2 Domain Name
The domain name has several parts and is mapped to an Internet Protocol (IP) address.
3 www
The vast majority of Web addresses have www (standing for World Wide Web) as the first part of the domain name.
4 Host
This part of the domain name is a name chosen by the owner of the website and can be, for example, a company name.

5 Type of site
This part of the domain tells you what type of site the website is. For example, .co or .com stand for commercial sites; .gov for government organizations; .org for non-profit organizations; and .edu or .ac for educational sites.
6 Country
Websites other than US sites also have a country code. UK denotes a website based in the United Kingdom.

INTERNET EXPLORER

Internet Explorer is one of the most popular Web-browsing programs and offers all the facilities that you need to browse the Web and become part of the online community.

WHAT CAN EXPLORER DO?

Internet Explorer comes as a standard part of Windows software and was probably already installed on your computer when it arrived. Explorer is more than just a Web-browsing program: it is a suite of programs offering a variety of Internet-related activities: from browsing the Web and composing and sending email, to taking the plunge and publishing your own Web pages. Outlook Express is the name of the email program that comes with Explorer, and FrontPage is Explorer's home Web-publishing program. Both these programs are the subject of their own books in this series, but a brief description is given here to help give you an idea of how the three programs are inter-related and what each can do.

WHAT IS EXPLORER?

Internet Explorer is the Web-browsing program that enables you to connect to websites and view them, surf the Web using hypertext links, and download files and programs from the Internet to your own computer. By default, its email features operate through Outlook Express, and its Edit feature is directly linked to Microsoft FrontPage.

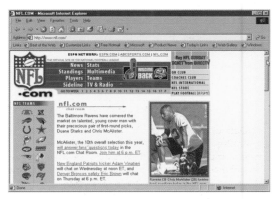

OUTLOOK EXPRESS

Outlook Express is an email program that enables you to perform all the activities necessary to send and receive email, manage your own online address book, and exchange files and information with friends over the Internet.

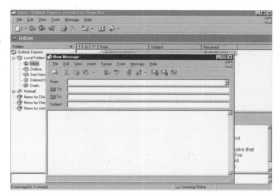

FRONTPAGE

The time may come when you want to create your own Web pages. FrontPage helps you to do just that. It provides a Web-page editor that enables you to build Web pages, with only a minimal understanding of HTML. You can then publish them live on the Web using your own computer as a Web server.

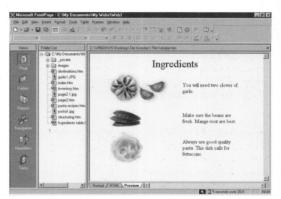

INSTALLING OTHER COMPONENTS

If Outlook Express or FrontPage are not on your computer, you can install them from your Windows or Internet Explorer CD-ROM. If you cannot locate your disks, another option open to you is to download a new version of Internet Explorer from the Microsoft website and reinstall the entire program on your computer, making sure that you elect to install these additional programs during the installation process. Click the Microsoft button on the Links bar to go to Microsoft's website.

LAUNCHING INTERNET EXPLORER

You can launch Internet Explorer directly from your computer's desktop or from the Windows Start menu by following the instructions below. Before you can actually connect to a website using Explorer you will need to connect to your Internet Service Provider. It does not matter whether you do this before or after starting Explorer. When Explorer starts running, it checks to see if it can find an active Internet connection. If it can't find a connection it will usually prompt you to make a connection. If Explorer is unable to make an automatic connection for any reason, you do not have to close the program and start again. You can connect manually to your service provider at any time while Explorer is running.

CONNECT TO YOUR SERVICE PROVIDER

• If you are using a dial-up connection, click on your Service Provider's dial-up networking connection and double-click.

• In the Connect To dialog box, type your user name and password.

• Click once on the Connect button to dial your Service Provider.

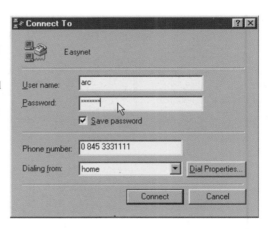

1 USING THE START MENU

• Click on Start on the Windows Taskbar to bring up the main menu.
• When Programs is highlighted and the pop-up programs menu appears, move across to highlight Internet Explorer.
• Click on Internet Explorer and the Explorer window opens .

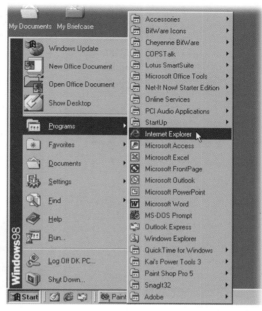

2 USING A SHORTCUT

• First, locate the Internet Explorer shortcut. This is a blue, graphically styled "e" with Internet written beneath it.
• When you have found it, position the mouse over the e and double-click to launch the Explorer program.
• The Explorer window appears .

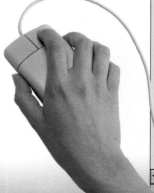

16 **The Explorer Window**

THE EXPLORER WINDOW

The Explorer main browser window opens automatically when you start Internet Explorer. It offers a selection of different toolbars, including a standard menu bar, an area for viewing Web pages and a status bar at the foot of the window. The status bar displays information relating to the transfer of pages and connectivity.

THE EXPLORER WINDOW

1 Title bar
The Title bar shows the title of the current Web page. It also tells you whether you are connected to the Internet or are working offline.

2 Menu bar
This shows the main menus that give you access to all Explorer's features.

3 Standard buttons
This toolbar contains all the main features you need to navigate around the Web.

4 Address bar
This is where you type the addresses of websites that you want to visit.

5 Links bar
This toolbar provides a selection of links to Microsoft-related websites.

6 Main browsing window
This area is where the websites that you visit will be displayed.

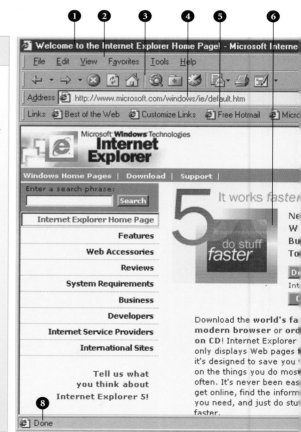

22 Using the Address Field

CROWDED TOOLBAR?

You can hide the labels on the Standard toolbar to make room for more buttons. Right-click on the toolbar and click Customize in the menu. In the Text options box of the Customize window, click the arrow and select No text labels. Click on Close.

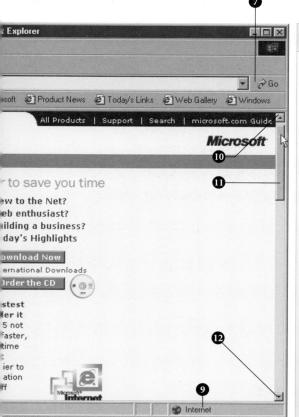

THE EXPLORER WINDOW

7 Go button
After typing the address of a website, using this button will request the page.

8 Status bar
This bar has information relating to the activity being carried out. For example, "Done" indicates that a requested Web page has been transferred to your Web browser, or, if you click on a hyperlink , the URL of that link will be displayed.

9 Connectivity icon
When you are working online, this icon is displayed.

10 Scroll-up arrow
Click on this arrow to move up the current Web page.

11 Scroll bar box
Drag this box in the scroll bar to see other parts of the current page quickly.

12 Scroll-down arrow
Click on this arrow to move down the current Web page.

23 Connecting to a site

25 Recognizing hypertext links

THE EXPLORER TOOLBARS

It is perfectly possible to use Internet Explorer using only the features provided on the standard buttons toolbar. This toolbar is at the top of the Explorer window and comprises a row of graphically styled buttons. These buttons are shortcuts to features that will help you find your way round the Web quickly, so it is worth spending time familiarizing yourself with the toolbar and learning what each symbol means. Each item on the toolbar is also in the main menus.

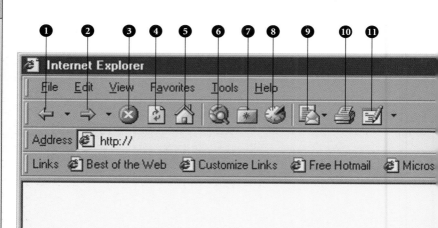

THE STANDARD TOOLBAR

1 Back
Takes you to the previous page you were on.
2 Forward
Displays the page on screen before using the Back button.
3 Stop
Stops a page downloading.

4 Refresh
Refreshes the current page to show the latest version.
5 Home
Loads the default home page.
6 Search
Opens the Search panel in the Explorer window. This gives you

access to features that help you connect to search engines.
7 Favorites
Opens the Favorites panel in the Explorer window, which allows you to create, access, and manage your favorite sites on the Web.

CUSTOMIZING A TOOLBAR

You might want to move the toolbars. To move the Links toolbar, place the cursor over the "handle," hold down the mouse button, the cursor becomes a double-headed arrow, then "drag" the bar to the preferred location.

ScreenTips

If you forget what any of the buttons on the toolbar do, all you have to do is click on the button and wait for a few seconds. A box appears with the button's name.

THE STANDARD TOOLBAR

8 History
Opens the History panel to the left in the Explorer window. This provides a list of websites that you have previously visited when using Explorer and by clicking one you can automatically connect to it.

9 Mail
Provides a menu of options related to email. These include opening a new email message and pasting the address of the current page into a new message.

10 Print
Prints the current page.

11 Edit
Allows you to edit the code of the current Web page, either in text form or using a Web page editor, such as FrontPage. Save any changes on your hard disk, but they will not affect the Web page itself.

29 **Opening the History Panel**

SAVING CONTENT

It is not possible for you to create or alter Web pages using the Internet Explorer browser. However, there will be many occasions when you come across screens containing information that you want to save, review later on, or to edit for your own personal use. Internet Explorer enables you to save text, images, and other files and programs onto your hard disk. Open a Web page that you would like to save for later use, and try some of the techniques described here.

1 SAVING A WEB PAGE

● To save an entire Web page to your hard disk, click on File in the menu bar and select Save As.
● In the Save Web Page dialog box, type the file name and click on Save.

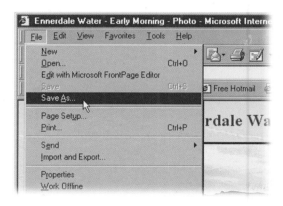

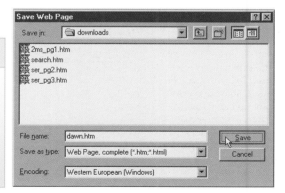

SAVING IMAGES AS WALLPAPER

If you see a striking image on a Web page, you can use Explorer to set it as your Windows wallpaper. Follow Step 2 (opposite), but choose Save As Wallpaper from the pop-up menu.

2 SAVING IMAGES

• Place the mouse cursor on the image that you want to save. Click the right mouse button to display a pop-up menu.

• Select Save Picture As and click with the left mouse button.

• In the Save Picture dialog box, navigate to the folder where you would like to save the file.

• Type a name in the File name box and click on the Save button.

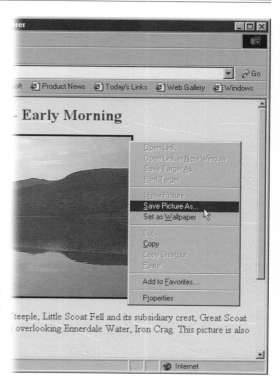

DOWNLOADING FROM WEB PAGES

Many Web pages contain files such as multimedia sound or video files, PDF files (Portable Document Files that can be viewed using Acrobat Reader), or computer programs. It is usually possible to save these files onto your hard disk. To save a file, follow Step 2 above and on the pop-up menu choose Save Target As, which will "live" on the menu. You will need the appropriate software to view or play the files that you save.

MOVING BETWEEN PAGES

Browsing, or "surfing," the Web is simply a process of opening a
Web page in your browser, identifying the "hot" elements on
that page and using them to move to another page.

USING THE ADDRESS FIELD

When you connect to your Service
Provider ⬚ and start Internet
Explorer your default home page ⬚
automatically opens in the browser
window ⬚. This page is likely to be a
Microsoft page or the home page of your
service provider. While it may contain
useful information for new users, soon
you will want to strike out and visit a site
of your choice, perhaps your company's
website or an international news site. You
do this by telling your computer the
address of the site you wish to visit. Find
the addresses of several sites you would
like to visit and try accessing them
following the instructions below.

1 CLEARING THE ADDRESS BAR
• Before you can type the
address of a site you must
first clear the current
contents of the address bar.
Position the mouse cursor
anywhere in the address
field and click once.
• The contents of the
address bar are highlighted.
• Press the ⬚← Bksp⬚ key to
delete the contents.

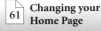
**Connecting to your
Service Provider** 14

**Changing your
Home Page** 61

**The Explorer
Window** 16

2 TYPING THE ADDRESS

You will notice that there is now a flashing insertion point in the address bar, ready for you to begin typing. Type the address as it appears, taking care to copy exactly all the punctuation and spelling.

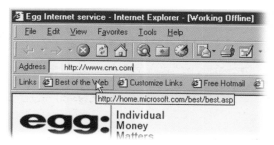

3 CONNECTING TO A SITE

Once you have typed the address, move the mouse cursor over the Go button, to the right of the address bar, and click once. Alternatively, you can also press the Enter⏎ key. Wait for a few moments while your computer contacts the remote computer you are calling. You can follow the progress of this call by watching the information in the Status bar at the foot of the browser window. Once the connection has been made, you will see the information in your browser window begin to change. When the Status bar says Done, the page has been fully downloaded to your computer.

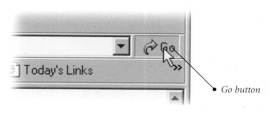

• Go button

4 EDITING AN ADDRESS

If you mistype the address or get it wrong, don't worry. Just as you can with a word processor, you can simply edit your mistakes.

• Position the mouse cursor after the character you wish to change and click the mouse button once. This will highlight the entire address, as in Step 1.

• Click again and the cursor will change to a flashing cursor ready for you to type any changes using the keyboard.

• When the address is correct, either click on the Go button or press `Enter ←`.

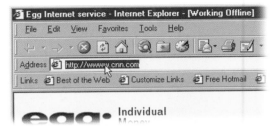

HAVING TROUBLE CONNECTING?

ℹ️ **The page cannot be displayed**

The page you are looking for is currently unavailable. The Web site might be experiencing technical difficulties, or you may need to adjust your browser settings.

There is a wide variety of reasons why you may experience difficulty connecting to a site. Servers sometimes go down and cannot be accessed. If you cannot get connected for this reason wait before trying again, but the wait can be anything from a few seconds to several hours. Another reason may be that you have mistyped the address. Check that the spelling and punctuation are correct and that no extra characters have crept in. Any slight discrepancy will prevent a connection.

FOLLOWING LINKS BETWEEN PAGES

Links are the very essence of the World Wide Web, and it is by following them that you can move from page to page without typing a new address each time. Links have several different guises, and learning to recognize their various forms will help you get the most from the Web. Hypertext links are the most common form and are displayed as text on the page, but graphic buttons and other images are increasingly used as a way of encouraging you to move to another page. Dorling Kindersley's website uses both types of links. Try identifying each of the types of links described here and following them using the instructions below.

RECOGNIZING HYPERTEXT LINKS

These are the most common and easily identified link. They are usually underlined and shown in a different color.
• Move the mouse cursor over the underlined text.
• If the cursor changes to a hand, the text is "hot."
• Click the mouse button once to follow that link.

VISITED LINKS

As you follow hypertext links within a single website you may start to notice two colors of links on the Web pages. This is because the links you have visited usually change color as a way of helping you keep track of where you have and have not been.

USING A NEW WINDOW

When you are browsing the Web, it can be useful to open a page in a new window so that you have two or more browser windows open at the same time. You can continue to explore one page while another is being downloaded. To open any link in a new window, place the mouse cursor over the link, right-click the mouse and choose Open Link in New Window from the pop-up menu that appears.

RECOGNIZING NAVIGATION BUTTONS

Many websites use graphically styled buttons as the main way of navigating around the site. These buttons often appear at the top, bottom, or side of a page.

• Move the mouse cursor over some of the different buttons.

• Wherever the cursor changes to a hand there is a link from that image.

• Click the mouse button once when you want to follow a particular link.

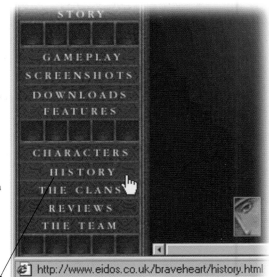

Navigation buttons

RECOGNIZING IMAGE LINKS

Some of the more design-conscious websites use image "maps" to provide links. These appear on the page as a single image, different parts of which link to different places. Often these images do not have text labels to act as signpost, which offers more exploratory and intuitive surfing. Again, the way to discover such links is to move the mouse cursor over the images and see if it changes to a hand.

NAVIGATING BACK AND FORTH

Following links is simple once you know how, but before long you may find that you have completely moved away from where you started, and are not sure how to get back. You may also have encountered a few interesting pages on the way but failed to note their addresses. How do you return to find them again? Internet Explorer provides several features that enable you to move between the pages you have visited. Open any Web page and follow between six and ten different links, then practice navigating using some of the techniques described below.

BACKWARDS AND FORWARDS PAGE BY PAGE

• Moving back is the most common operation you'll perform. To move back to the previous page you visited, place the cursor over the Back button on the toolbar and click once. Repeat the process to move back through several pages.
• To move forward to a page you were on before

you pressed Back, place the cursor over the Forward button and click once.

Repeat the process to move forward to the most recent page you opened.

BACK USING THE MENU

• To move back to any page you have visited in the current session, position the mouse cursor over the arrow to the right of the Back button and click once. Select the page you wish to return to from the drop-down menu that appears.

FORWARD
USING THE MENU

• To move forward to any page that you accessed in the current session before you used the Back feature, position the mouse pointer over the arrow to the right of the Forward button and click once.

• Select the page you wish to return to from the drop-down menu that appears.

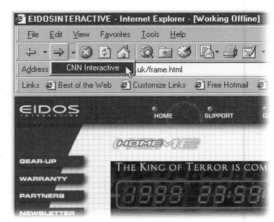

USING THE ADDRESS MENU

Explorer makes its own list of sites you visit regularly or access specifically by typing the address. You can access any of the sites on this list by positioning the mouse over the arrow at the end of the address bar and clicking once. A drop-down menu will appear. Use the scroll bar to see the full list. Position the mouse cursor over the address of interest and click once to promote that address into the address bar. If a connection is not made automatically, click Go or press the [Enter ←] key to make the connection.

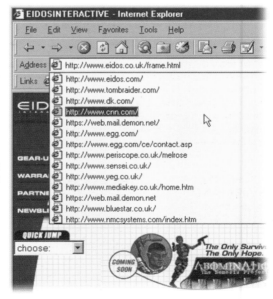

USING THE GO TO MENU

The Go To menu provides a list of all the sites you have visited in the current session, regardless of whether they came before or after the page you are currently on. To access this menu, click on View in the menu bar and select Go To. The list of sites appears in the lowest section of the drop-down submenu. Position the mouse cursor over the site you wish to access and click once.

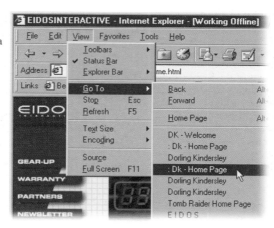

USING THE BROWSING HISTORY

Another means of accessing websites that you have already visited is to use Internet Explorer's History feature. This maintains a record of all the websites that you have visited during the current session as well as over the last few days or weeks. You can specify how many days you would like

Explorer to keep items in its History, and you can also clear all items from this memory whenever you wish to start afresh. Once you have visited a few websites, open the History panel and try returning to a site you visited earlier by following these instructions.

OPENING THE HISTORY PANEL

• To see a list of all the items stored in History, position the mouse cursor over the History button on the main toolbar and click once. The History panel will open inside the Explorer window.

OPEN A PAGE
IN THE LIST

• Position the mouse cursor over any page in the list so that it turns into a hand. A drop-down list appears showing the pages in that site you have visited. Click once to open the page you want in the main browser window.

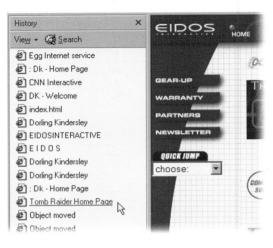

Sorting the History

You can sort the History pages by clicking the small arrow to the right of the View button in the History bar. A drop-down menu appears from which you can select to sort by date, site, the most visited, or in the order the pages have been visited today.

CHANGING THE
LENGTH OF TIME
SITES REMAIN IN
HISTORY

• Click on the Tools menu and select Internet Options. The Internet Options dialog box opens showing the General settings.

• At the bottom of this page is the History subsection. To change the number of days for which History will remember sites, position the mouse cursor in the box to the right of Days to keep pages in history, and double-click to select the number in the box. When it is highlighted, type the required number of days. Click on the OK button at the foot of the dialog box.

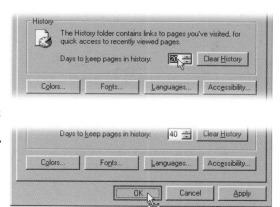

CLEARING THE HISTORY

• Open the Internet Options box as described opposite. Position the mouse cursor over the Clear History button in the History panel and then click the OK button to close the box.

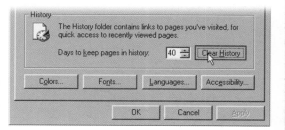

CLOSING THE HISTORY PANEL

• Position the mouse cursor over the X on the History bar and click once.

SEARCHING THE WEB

The Web has a variety of sophisticated search tools, called search engines, which exist purely to help you find your way around the billions of pages stored on computers worldwide.

SEARCHING WITH EXPLORER

Explorer has a Search Assistant that enables you to search for websites, companies, email addresses, and other information according to keywords or phrases that you type. Connect to your Internet Service Provider, then try searching with the Assistant, following the procedures illustrated here.

USING THE SEARCH ASSISTANT

● Position the mouse cursor over the Search button on the toolbar and click once. The Search panel will open to the left of the main window and the Search Assistant page will be displayed.

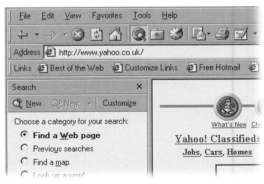

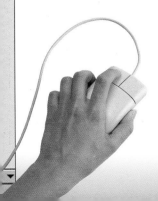

• Choose the type of search you want by clicking the mouse over your preferred option in the list.

• Click the mouse in the search box and type your keyword(s). Position the mouse cursor over the Search button and click once to start your search.

• The results will appear in the search panel after a few seconds. Use the scroll bar to browse the full list.

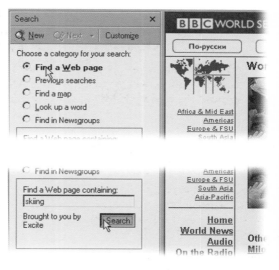

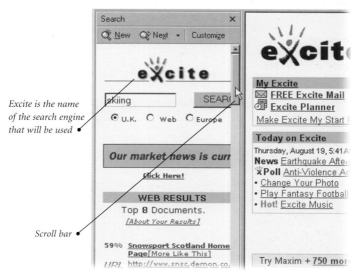

Excite is the name of the search engine that will be used •

Scroll bar •

• Position the mouse cursor over the title of any site in the list and click once to open that page.
• The page appears in the main browser window.

SAME SEARCH, DIFFERENT ENGINE

• If your search does not return any satisfactory matches, try running it again through a different search engine using the Next feature.
• Position the mouse cursor over the black arrow to the right of the Next button in the Search panel. Click to bring up a menu of other search engines.
• Position the mouse cursor over the engine of your choice and click the mouse to select it.

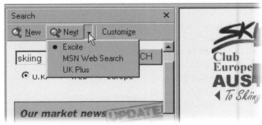

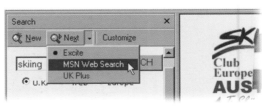

• A new search page will appear in the Search panel. A different set of results is displayed once you have reentered your keyword(s) and clicked on Search.

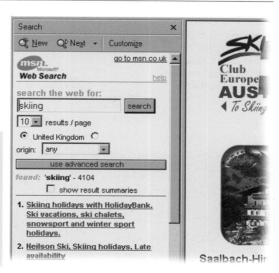

Ending a download
If you begin to download a page that you've found via a search, you may soon decide that it's not what you're interested in. A quick way to end a download is to press the [Esc] key.

CUSTOMIZING THE SEARCH ASSISTANT

Once you have established how you prefer to search, you can customize the way the Search Assistant looks and works to suit you.
• Open the Customize Search Settings box by positioning the mouse cursor over the Customize button in the Search menu bar and clicking once.

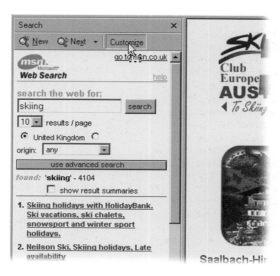

ADDING OR REMOVING SEARCH CATEGORIES

● You can add or remove categories from the Search Assistant page by clicking the mouse cursor in the check box next to a category. Click once to remove (and again to add) a check mark.

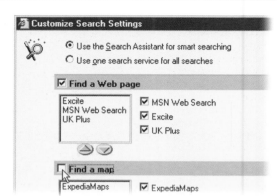

ADDING OR REMOVING OPTIONS

● You can add or remove options from a category list by clicking the mouse cursor in the relevant check boxes, as above.

CHANGING THE ORDER OF OPTIONS

● To change the order of items in a list, select the item you want to move by clicking the mouse over it, then click the up or down arrows to promote or demote the item.

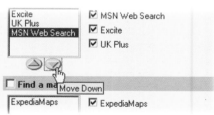

START SEARCHING

It is also possible to begin a Web search directly from the Window's Start menu. Click on the Start button, select Find, and then click On the Internet. This will launch Internet Explorer and the Search Assistant. The new search may open in a small panel on your screen, which you can then maximize.

PERFORMING AN AUTOSEARCH

Explorer also allows you to perform an autosearch directly from the Address Bar  without opening the Search panel.

● Position the mouse cursor in the address bar and click once to highlight the text already there.

● Type the word Go, or Find, followed by a space and then the word or phrase you wish to search for. Press the [Enter ←] key to execute the search, and wait for the results to appear in the Search panel.

● Any matches will be displayed in the Search panel as a list of hyperlinks, which you can click on to view the sites in the main Explorer window.

Internet Explorer could not find any web address matches for your query.

Please refer to the Autosearch matches in the search bar at the left or click the ⇐ Back button to return to the Web site you were viewing.

This message is displayed if there is no exact URL to match your search term.

Choosing a Search Tool

The Web has a host of search sites you can use, each drawing on its own database of information. Explorer's Search Assistant accesses several different search engines, but if your search is obscure, you may have to cast your net a bit wider. There are many other search tools that you can try, some of which specialize in certain types of information, such as email addresses or newsgroups. To search effectively, it pays to match your search tool to the type of information you want to find, and to understand the nature of your search. Are you looking for all sites related to a particular subject, or do you seek a specific person or company, for example?

WEB DIRECTORIES

Web directories are lists of subject categories and subcategories that you can browse through looking for websites. Using a directory is rather like looking up a telephone number in the yellow pages. It gives you all the entries in a particular category, but in order to find the information, you have to know where to look for it. Consequently, directories are most helpful when you are looking for general information by subject or by an activity.

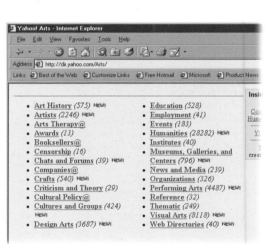

DIRECTORY ADDRESSES

Here are the addresses of some of the more popular Web directories:

Yellow Pages . . www.yellowpages.com
Yahoo! . . . . www.yahoo.com
Magellan . . . . . magellan.mckinley.com
Galaxy . . . . galaxy.einet.net

SEARCH ENGINES

Here are the addresses of some of the more popular search engines:

www.altavista.com   www.lycos.com
www.dogpile.com   www.yahoo.com
www.excite.com   webcrawler.com
www.hotbot.com   infoseek.go.com

32   Using the Search Assistant

SEARCH ENGINES

Search engines offer more powerful searching facilities than Web directories, and will search the Web according to the information you give them by using keywords and other information including language and country. The search engines match your search criteria to Web pages that are listed in their index, and return a list of "hits," or matches, with your search criteria. The most relevant matches are listed first. You can then view the matched sites by following hyperlinks 🗋. The AltaVista search engine has a huge database and offers multilingual searches. Results are usually returned within a matter of seconds.

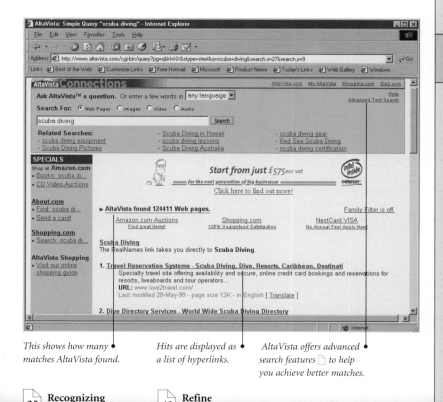

This shows how many • matches AltaVista found.

Hits are displayed as • a list of hyperlinks.

AltaVista offers advanced • search features 🗋 to help you achieve better matches.

25 Recognizing Hypertext Links

43 Refine Your Search

Searching Tips

There are no hard and fast rules about Web searching, and it can be one of the most frustrating activities. Even with all the millions of websites to choose from, many people complain of not being able to find anything on the Web. There are many reasons it can be difficult: there is no universal index of websites; sites tend to be registered by developers rather than editors, so the information given to the databases is not always very helpful; and each search engine logs different information and operates in a slightly different way from its counterparts. So, although there are some general tips and guidelines that will help you search more effectively, you will find that there is no substitute for taking the time to explore the specific hints and instructions offered on each individual search site.

READ THE INSTRUCTIONS

Most of the search engines contain clear, precise instructions on how to search. Spend some time reading these. They can usually be accessed via a hyperlink or help button that is part of the search engine's home page.

• The NorthernLight search engine has simple, clear instructions that are accessed by clicking Help on the home page.

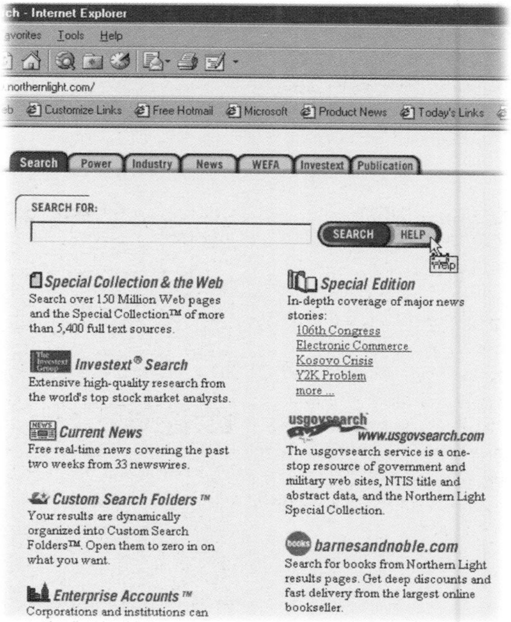

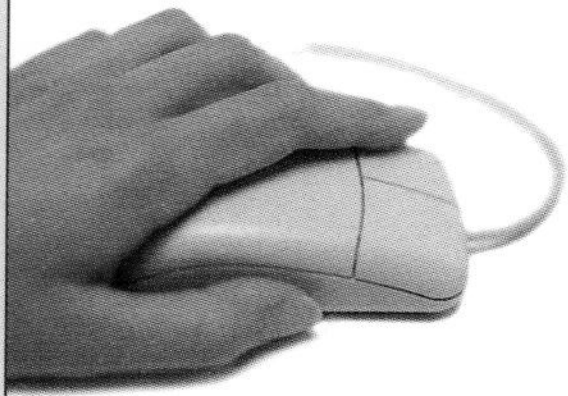

25 Recognizing Hypertext Links

• The instructions tell you that you can also ask questions, such as "What is the capital of Sweden?"

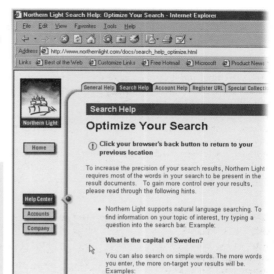

Try again...
If you have no luck with one search engine or directory, try running the same search on an alternative engine; they use different databases of websites.

USE MULTIPLE KEYWORDS

Using more than one keyword makes a search more specific. If seeking novels by a particular author, for example, the keywords "books" and "faulks" are more likely to produce useful results than using either word by itself. Separate different keywords with spaces.

SEARCH FOR EXACT PHRASES

When using two keywords, the search engine finds sites that contain both keywords. A search for White House is as likely to find sites about white-painted houses as well as the presidential residence. Putting quotation marks around "White House" tells the engine to look for that exact phrase.

SEARCHING FOR PEOPLE

With the ever-increasing popularity of email, being able to find people on the Internet is becoming as important as finding websites. There are several excellent people finding directories that list e-mail addresses and residential listings.

InfoSpace . . . . www.infospace.com
AnyWho . . . . www.anywho.com
Switchboard . . . . www.switchboard.com
WhoWhere? . . . . www.whowhere.com
Yahoo!: People Search . . . . www.people.yahoo.com

USE LOGICAL OPERATORS

Most search engines understand logical expressions, such as AND, OR, or NOT. They help to narrow down a search. When used between one or more keywords, these expressions have the following meanings: NEAR looks for pages where the adjacent keywords occur close together; AND looks for pages where instances of both words occur; OR looks for pages where there are instances of either keyword; NOT looks for pages where there are instances of the word preceding NOT, but not the word following it.

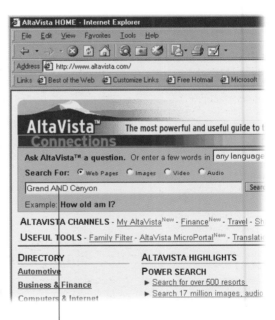

Logical operators are placed between keywords when searching.

REFINE YOUR SEARCH

Many search engines allow you to refine your search using advanced search criteria. You may be able to specify the language, country, and type of website you are looking for. The exact criteria will vary from engine to engine, so it is best to try out several sites to find the one that best suits you.

• On the Lycos home page, you can refine your search at the bottom of a page of hits.

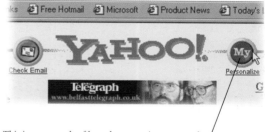

<< . **1** . <u>2</u> . <u>3</u> . <u>4</u> . <u>5</u> . <u>6</u> . <u>7</u> . <u>8</u> . <u>9</u> . <u>10</u> . <u>>></u>

Search ⦿ **Refine your search** or ⦾ **New Sear**

for | salsa london |

| all the words (any order) | in | The Web

Display | 10 ▾ | Results   Find !   All Se
Options
10
20
30
40

➤➤ Go Online Free

Copyright © 1998 Lycos, Inc. All Rights Reserved.
Lycos® is a registered trademark of Carnegie Mellon University.

SET YOUR SEARCH PREFERENCES

Many of the big search engines enable you to customize their search pages so that you do not have to select your search options each time you use that search engine. Once you have found an advanced search formula that works, you can tell the search engine to remember the preferences for you.

• On some sites you can access the customize page from the My button on the home page. You can choose a user name and password, and you then have the option to select your preferred search criteria.

🔗 Free Hotmail   🔗 Microsoft   🔗 Product News   🔗 Today's

Check Email   **YAHOO!**   My
Personalize

Telegraph
www.belfasttelegraph.co.uk

This is an example of how the customize page can be accessed from the My button on the home page.

BOOKMARK YOUR FAVORITE SEARCH TOOLS

If you become a regular Internet user you are likely to return to at least one of the search engines on a regular basis. It is useful to bookmark your favorite search sites so that you are able to access them quickly whenever you wish.

FAVORITES

Internet Explorer provides a way for you to create a digital bookmark for any site as a "favorite," which adds it to a special list that you can access quickly and easily whenever you wish.

THE FAVORITES PANEL

One of the features of Internet Explorer is a window that you can have open all the time on the left-hand side of the main browser window. It is called the Favorites panel, and from this panel you can access and organize your collection of favorites.

Explorer provides some suggested favorite places to get you started. Once you have connected to the Internet, you can try accessing some favorites using the Favorites panel and some of the other methods described in this chapter.

OPENING THE FAVORITES PANEL

• Position the mouse cursor over the Favorites button on the main toolbar and click once.
• The Favorites panel will open on screen in the left-hand side of the main Explorer window.

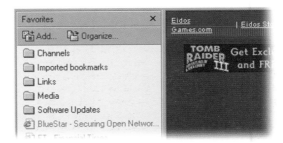

OPENING A FAVORITE SITE

• In the Favorites panel, position the mouse cursor over the site that you wish to open. When the cursor turns into a hand, click once to open that site in the main window.

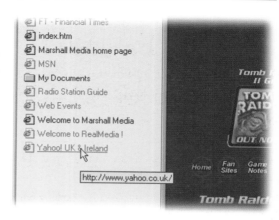

CLOSING THE FAVORITES PANEL

• When you have finished using your favorites, you can close the Favorites panel by positioning the mouse cursor over the X in the Favorites bar and clicking once. The main browser window expands to fill the available space.

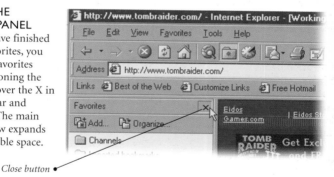

Close button •

OPENING A FAVORITE USING THE FAVORITES MENU

You can also access your favorites directly from the Favorites menu. The advantage of using the menu instead of the panel is that you have a larger window area in which to view the Web pages you select. To open a favorite using this method, position the mouse cursor over the Favorites menu and click once. A drop-down menu will appear, listing all your current favorites. Move the mouse cursor over the one of interest (submenus appear next to folders). When it becomes highlighted click the mouse once to open it.

CREATING YOUR OWN FAVORITES

As your experience of finding your way around the World Wide Web increases, it is inevitable that you will accumulate a selection of sites that you refer to more than any others: your preferred search engine, news providers, your bank, particular companies, and sites offering a little light relief, for example. These sites are the perfect candidates to be your favorite places. Adding one of these sites to your favorites is very simple and can be done by using the Favorites panel or via the Favorites menu, depending on how you prefer to use your browser. Connect to the Internet and open a site that you would like to add to your favorite places. Then follow the instructions below, using whichever method you prefer.

1 CREATING USING FAVORITES PANEL

• Position the mouse cursor over the Favorites button on the main toolbar and click once to display the Favorites panel on screen.
• In the Favorites panel, position the mouse cursor over the Add button and click once. Now go to Step 3.

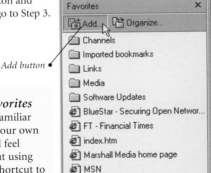

Add button

Keyboard favorites
Once you are familiar with creating your own favorites, you'll feel confident about using the keyboard shortcut to creating a favorite, which is to hold down the [Ctrl] key and press D.

39 Search Engines

2 CREATING USING FAVORITES MENU

• Alternatively, position the mouse cursor over Favorites on the menu bar and click once to activate the Favorites menu. Position the mouse cursor over Add to Favorites and click once when it becomes highlighted.

3 NAMING A FAVORITE

• The Add Favorite dialog box will now open and the name of the favorite you have just created will be shown in the Name box. If you would like to change the name, position the mouse cursor after the text in the Name box and click once. A flashing insertion point will appear. Press the ← Bksp key and hold it down until all the text has been deleted.

• Now type your preferred name for this favorite. If you wish to store the favorite in a particular folder go to Step 4, otherwise click on OK.

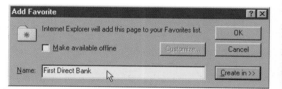

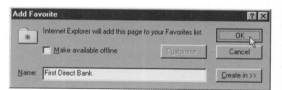

4 FILING A FAVORITE

• In the Add Favorite box, click the Create in>> button to open the Favorites directory. Navigate to the folder you wish to store the favorite in. Double-click on the folder to open it and single-click on a folder to select it.

• When you have selected the folder, position the mouse cursor over the OK button at the top and click once to save the favorite in the chosen folder.

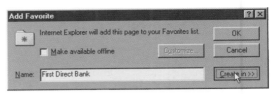

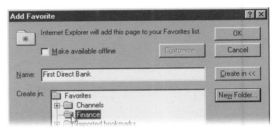

MAKING FAVORITES AVAILABLE OFFLINE

If you access some of your favorite places frequently, you can make them available for offline browsing. This means that the page will be saved locally on your computer and you will not need to connect to your service provider every time you want to see it. This will save your phone bills, but it will also mean that if the site is updated often you may not have the latest information. To make a page available for viewing offline, position the mouse cursor over the favorite and right-click. Place the mouse cursor over Choose Make Available Offline from the pop-up menu and left-click.

ORGANIZING YOUR FAVORITES

You will find that your list of favorites grows very quickly, and you may find it helpful to create a structured filing system for them so that you can easily find the things you are looking for. You can do this with folders in much the same way that you organize any other files that you store on your computer. Because the Web is changing all the time, you may also find occasions when you go to a favorite only to discover that it no longer exists. It is easy to delete an obsolete favorite from the list. All these functions can be managed from the Organize Favorites box. This box can be accessed from the Favorites menu or the Favorites panel.

1 ORGANIZING IN FAVORITES PANEL

• Position the mouse cursor over the Favorites button on the main toolbar and click once.

• Position the mouse cursor over the Organize button in the Favorites panel and click once.

• The Organize Favorites box will open.

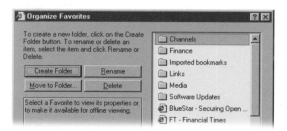

2 ORGANIZING IN FAVORITES MENU

• Position the mouse cursor over Favorites on the menu bar and click once.
• Position the mouse cursor over Organize Favorites and click once.
• The Organize Favorites box will open.

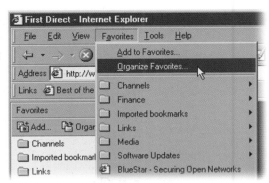

CREATING A NEW FOLDER

• To create a new folder on the top level simply click the Create Folder button. A new folder will appear in the list on the right.
• Type the name of the folder and then press the [Enter ←] key.
• To create a folder within another folder click on the folder in the list on the right so that it becomes highlighted.

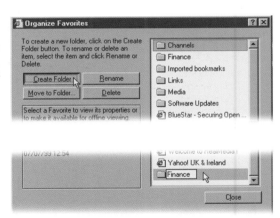

• Now click the Create Folder button. Then type the name as opposite.

MOVING A FAVORITE

• To move a favorite from one folder to another, click on the favorite in the list on the right so that it is highlighted.
• Click the Move to Folder button. The Browse for Folder window will open.

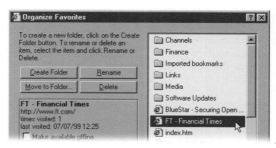

Drag and drop

If you can see the location to which you want to move a favorite, you can place the cursor over it, hold down the mouse button and "drag" it to the new location where it can be "dropped."

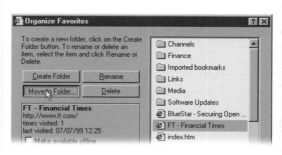

• Navigate to the folder you wish to store the favorite in, double-click on a folder to open it and single-click on a folder to select it.

• When you have selected the folder, position the mouse cursor over the OK button and click once to move the favorite to the chosen folder.

DELETING A FAVORITE

• To delete a favorite, click on the favorite in the list on the right so that it is highlighted.

• Position the mouse cursor over the Delete button and click once.

• Click Yes in the Confirm File Delete box to delete the favorite. The favorite will disappear from the list.

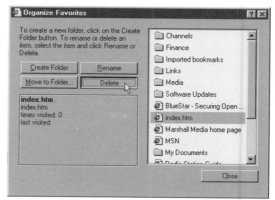

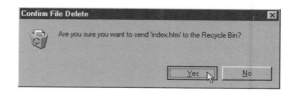

RENAMING A FAVORITE

• To rename a favorite, click on the favorite in the list on the right so that it is highlighted.

• Position the mouse cursor over the Rename button and click once. The name of the favorite will become highlighted in a box that you can edit.

• Type in the new name and press the [Enter ←] key when you have finished. You will see the name change in the list.

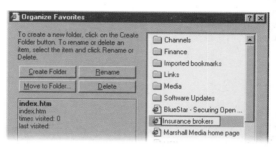

CLOSING THE ORGANIZE BOX

• When you have finished, close the Organize Favorites box by positioning the mouse cursor over the Close button and clicking.

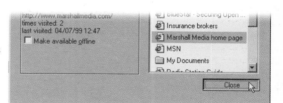

USING THE RIGHT MOUSE BUTTON

With the Favorites panel open in the browser window, you can perform several of the activities shown here, such as deleting and renaming, directly from the panel by using the right mouse button. Position the mouse cursor over any favorite and click the right mouse button once. You will see a pop-up menu with Delete and Rename as options. Move the mouse cursor over the desired option and click the left mouse button to activate it. If you choose Delete, you will be asked to confirm the action. Click Yes to proceed. If you select Rename, a text box that you can edit will appear. Type the new name and press the [Enter ←] key when you have finished.

PERSONALIZING

Internet Explorer is configured using Microsoft's default settings. However, it is possible to personalize the way Internet Explorer looks and works to suit your own preferences.

THE INTERNET OPTIONS WINDOW

The Internet Options window is where you can change Explorer's default settings. It allows you to change aspects such as display settings, security features, connection details, content control, storage of Internet files by the cache (an area of temporary memory on your hard disk) and other features. There are also major changes you can make when you have more experience. Most of the settings referred to in this chapter can be changed using the Internet Options window.

OPENING INTERNET OPTIONS WINDOW FROM THE MENU

• Position the mouse cursor over Tools on the main menu and click once to open the Tools menu. Highlight Internet Options on the menu and click once to open the Internet Options window.

USING THE RIGHT MOUSE BUTTON

• Position the mouse cursor over the Explorer icon on the desktop. Click the right mouse button, highlight Properties from the pop-up menu that appears and click the left mouse button to open the Internet Options window.

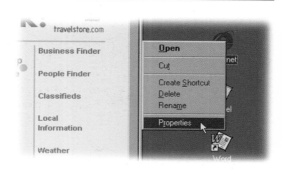

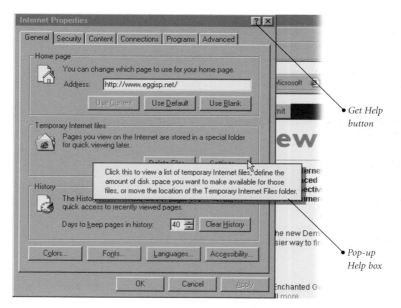

Get Help button

Pop-up Help box

HELP WITH INTERNET OPTIONS

• If you are not sure what an Internet Option does, you can get help by clicking on the question mark at top right of the Internet Options window. A question mark is attached to the cursor, which you can then move to the option you need help with and clicking once. A Help box pops up telling you about that option.

SAVING YOUR OPTIONS

• When you have made any changes to the Internet Options, click on the OK button to save the changes. Click Cancel if you do not want to save the changes.

CHANGING THE DISPLAY SETTINGS

Web designers often specify the color, size and font for text, the color of links, and background color as part of an integral design of their sites. If you cannot read the text easily, you can override the default settings of the page. The downside is that the look of Web pages may be adversely affected. Text may not flow neatly around images, and some images may appear transparent or fuzzy when viewed against a background color they were not designed for. However, you can choose to use your preferred settings all the time, or only when a design has not been specified.

CHANGING FONT SIZE FROM THE MENU

You can increase or decrease the size of the text used on Web pages.

• Click on View in the menu bar and highlight Text Size. A submenu appears.

• Move the cursor over your preferred option and click with the left mouse button.

• The setting you choose will remain in force until you change it again.

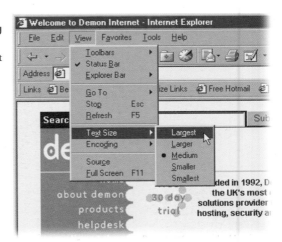

CHOOSING THE TYPEFACE

Under the General tab of Internet Options you can choose which font, or typeface, you would like Internet Explorer to use. The font you choose will be used when a typeface has not been specified in a Web page as part of its design. To choose a font, first open the Internet Options window 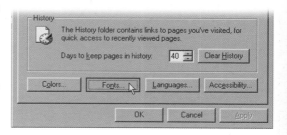, place the cursor over the General tab, click once to bring it to the front, and follow these instructions.

• Click the Fonts button at the foot of the window to open the Fonts box.
• In the Fonts dialog box use the scroll bars to find your preferred font, place the cursor over it and click to highlight it, then click the OK button to select it and return to Internet Options.
• Save your options 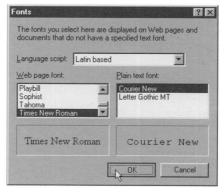 to apply the new settings.

CHOOSING HYPERLINK COLORS

You can specify the colors that display normal text, and for unvisited and visited hyperlinks □. You can also choose a "hover" color. If you choose a hover color, a hyperlink changes to that color when you roll the cursor over that link.

SETTING A COLOR

• Whether you want to set a text, hyperlink, or a background color, begin by opening the Internet Options window □ and click on the General tab to bring it to the front if it is not already displayed.

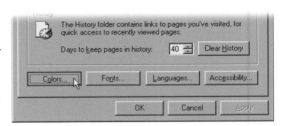

• Click the Colors button at the foot of the window to open the Colors dialog box.

• In the Colors dialog box click the mouse in the Use Window colors check box to remove the check mark if there is one in the box.

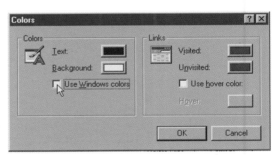

• Click the color box next to either Text or Background, depending on which of the two settings you want to change.

• Click on your preferred color in the color palette, then click on OK. When you want to return to the default text color, simply put a check mark back in the Use Window colors check box.

• Change the visited and unvisited hyperlink colors by following the same process in the Links panel.

• To set a hover color, click the mouse in the Use hover color check box and then click on the color button next to Hover. Select your preferred color from the color palette as before.
• Click on the OK button at the bottom to leave the Color dialog box, then save your options to apply the changes.

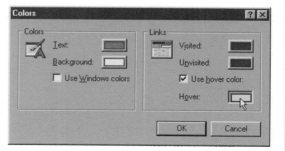

OVERRIDING PAGE DISPLAY SETTINGS

The font and color settings that you choose are only used if a Web page does not specify these options in its design, but with Web developers becoming ever more design conscious, most now tend to specify fonts, font sizes, and colors. If you would prefer to use your settings all the time when using the Web, you can elect to override the design style of the page using

Explorer's Accessibility options. These Accessibility options are found under the General tab of the Internet Options. You can choose to override Web page font, background color, and font point size settings, or only a selection of these features. First, open the Internet Options window and click the mouse over the General tab to bring it to the front.

• Click the Accessibility button at the bottom of the window to open the Accessibility dialog box.
• Place the cursor over the check box next to the option you want to set and click to place a check mark in the box. Then click on OK to close the Accessibility box.
• Save your options to apply the changes.

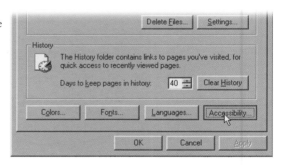

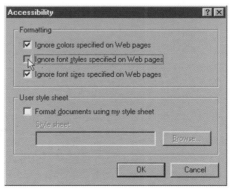

| 54 | The Internet Options Window |

| 56 | Saving your Options |

CHANGING YOUR HOME PAGE

The home page is the page that opens each time you start Internet Explorer. When you first install Explorer, the home page is usually configured to open Microsoft's website. There may well be information of interest to you on Microsoft's site, but it is more likely to be of only occasional interest. The ideal home page would be a page that you will want to open each time you connect. It might be a useful jumping off point or source of information you require regularly. The page you choose will depend mainly on how you use the Web. Among the possible contenders as your home page might be your favorite search engine, news site, share tracker, bookstore, game site, chat site, your Internet Service Provider, or email access on the Web. Changing the home page is simple and can be done from the General tab in the Internet Options window.

• In the Home Page section of the Internet Options dialog box, double-click the mouse in the Address field to highlight the address of your current home page, and type the address of your new home page.

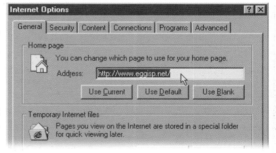

• You can click Use Current if you want to use your home page as the Web page that is currently displayed behind the Internet Options dialog box.
• Save your options to apply the changes. This page now appears when you start Internet Explorer or when you click the Home button on the toolbar.

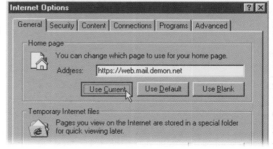

MANAGING THE CACHE

The cache is an area of temporary memory on your hard disk where Explorer stores temporary Internet files. These are transferred to your computer when you request a Web page. They display the Web page and include the image, text, and multimedia files. Explorer stores these files so that time can be saved by loading the page from the hard disk if you revisit the page. You may want to clear the cache to save space, you may want to open a page from the cache, or tell Explorer how often to compare a cached page to one on the Web. These instructions show you how.

CLEARING THE CACHE

• You access the cache by first opening the Internet options window and clicking the General tab.
• Position the mouse over the Delete Files button in the Temporary Internet files section to clear the cache of these temporary Internet files.

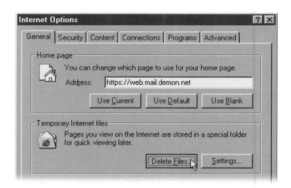

OPENING THE CACHE SETTINGS

• Position the cursor over the Settings button to open the Settings dialog box and click once.

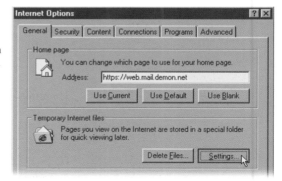

The dialog box options
determine how often
Explorer checks the cache.

• Choose Every visit to the
page if you want to make
sure you always have the
most recent version of a
Web page.

• Click the View Files
button to see a list of files
stored in the cache. You can
open any of these files in
Explorer by double-clicking
them with the mouse.

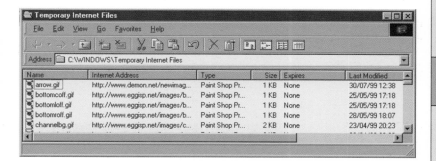

• Click OK to leave the
Settings box. Save your
options to apply the
changes you have made.

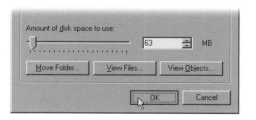

HANDLING MULTIMEDIA FILES

If you are using the Internet with a slow modem connection, you may decide not to download images and other multimedia files because they slow down the speed at which a Web page is downloaded to your computer. Explorer lets you specify which types of files to turn off in the Advanced section of Internet Options.

• Open the Internet Options window and click on the Advanced tab to bring it to the front.
• Use the scroll bar to scroll down until the Multimedia icon is at the top of the window.
• If you want to disable any multimedia files, and they are already checked, click the mouse in the check box next to the relevant options from Play animations, Play Sounds, Play videos, and Show pictures.
• Save your options to apply the changes.

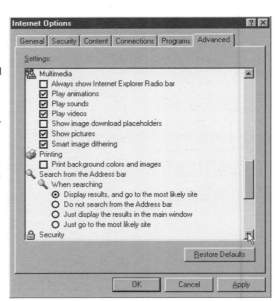

MULTIMEDIA PLUG-INS

Internet Explorer 5 comes with three multimedia "plug-in" programs pre-installed: Shockwave, Flash, and RealPlayer. These plug-ins enable you to view most of the animations, sound files, and videos used on the Internet. If a Web page requires a different plug-in, you will be prompted to install it. This is usually just a process of downloading the software and installing it, then returning to the Web page to see what it has to offer.

| 54 | The Internet Options Window | | 56 | Saving your Options |

CHOOSING PROGRAMS

Explorer provides its own email and newsreading facilities, in the shape of the Outlook Express program, but if you already have email or newsreading programs installed on your computer, your can opt to use those programs instead of Outlook Express. By setting your program preferences, you are able to access your other programs directly when you choose email or News from Explorer's Tools menu. Follow these instructions to set up the available program options. First, open the Internet Options dialog box and click the Programs tab.

• Choose your preferred option for each of these program types by clicking the arrows to view a list of programs to choose from. Select a program by moving the mouse, highlighting, and clicking on the desired program.
• Click OK to save your chosen options.

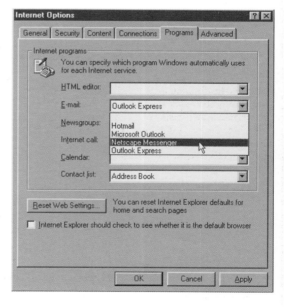

SETTING UP SECURITY

With the global expansion of electronic commerce, and money changing hands over the Internet around the clock, online security is an important issue, but one that can only be touched on here. Internet Explorer provides several types of security settings. It allows you to set the level of risk that you are prepared to take when receiving data over the Internet. For example, how likely is the data to harm your computer with a virus? It also offers control over the type of content you receive; and it has features that enable you to identify secure and trusted websites. This is particularly important since the advent of online shopping.

SETTING THE ZONE AND LEVEL

The Internet Option Security tab enables you to categorize particular websites into various zones, such as trusted or restricted, and set the level of security you would like to operate across each zone, such as high or low security risk. You may want to set up this security for "secure" websites where you can shop or send confidential information. To set up the security for a zone, follow this sequence:

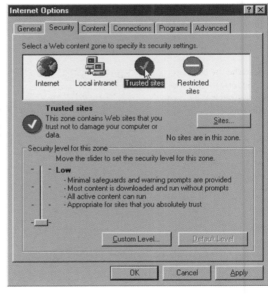

• Position the mouse cursor over the relevant icon in the top panel and click to highlight it.
• Click on the Sites button to add a site to that zone (this option is only available for the Trusted and Restricted zones).

• The Trusted sites dialog box opens. Type the address of the website you would like to add in the Add this webSite to the zone field, then click OK.

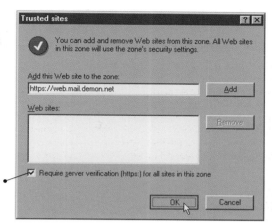

Check this box if you want this zone to include "secure" websites, that are prefixed by https:// only.

• Use the mouse to drag the Security Level slider to the desired position (you will see the name of the level change as you move the slider).
• Click OK to save your changes or repeat the sequence for another zone.

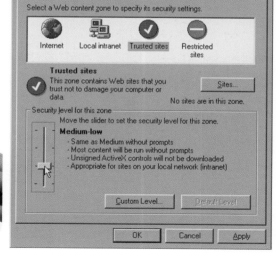

CONTROLLING CONTENT

As well as being the home to millions of interesting sites, the Web is also fertile ground for pornography and many other forms of unauthorized, offensive, and illegal information. To prevent your Web browser from being used to view sites that contain this kind of material, you can use Explorer's Content Advisor features. These enable you to censor sites that feature bad language, nudity, sex, and violence.

• First, open the Internet Options window ⬚ and click the Content tab.
• In the Content Advisor dialog box, click on the Enable button.

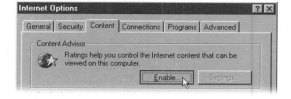

• On the Ratings tab, click on and highlight the type of content that you want to control in the Select a category window.

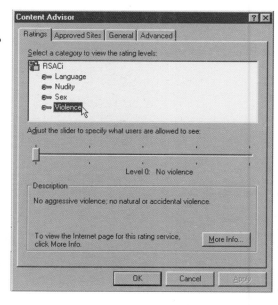

• Drag the slider across to the desired level of access (you will see information about the levels as you move the slider).

• Repeat this process for each of the content types you want to control.

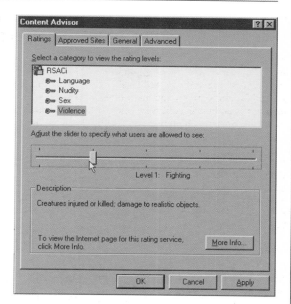

• Click the OK button.

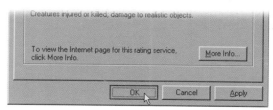

• Type your password in both fields of the Create Supervisor Password box. (Remember to make a note of this somewhere safe!) Now click on OK.

• Your content security is now set up and only you, as the holder of the password, can alter the settings.

GLOSSARY

CHANNEL
Website designed to deliver content to your computer. If you are running active desktop in Windows '98 you can access channel websites directly from the desktop, without using Internet Explorer.

DOWNLOAD
Transferring data from one computer to another. Your browser downloads HTML code and graphics to display a page.

EMAIL (ELECTRONIC MAIL)
The system for sending electronic messages between computers.

FAVORITES
Website for which you have created an electronic "bookmark" enabling you to access it from the Favorite menu in the toolbar.

GIF (GRAPHICS INTERCHANGE FORMAT)
A widely used file format for Web-based images.

HOME PAGE
The first page you see when you arrive at a website and typically contains a welcome message and hyperlinks to other pages.

HTML (HYPERTEXT MARKUP LANGUAGE)
A computer language used to create Web pages. HTML consists of a number of tags that describe how a page should be displayed.

HYPERTEXT
A term used to refer to the technique of linking pages together with hyperlinks.

HYPERLINK
A shortcut to another Web page. You click on a hyperlink to jump to its target.

INTERNET
The network of interconnected computers that communicate using the TCP/IP protocol.

INTERNET SERVICE PROVIDER
A business that provides a connection to the Internet.

JPEG (JOINT PHOTO-GRAPHIC EXPERTS GROUP)
A file format for Web-based images, particularly for photographic images.

MODEM
A device used to connect to the Internet over a telephone line.

NETWORK
A collection of computers that are linked together.

NEWSGROUP
A discussion group on the Internet where people exchange comments and other information.

OFFLINE
Not connected to the Internet.

ONLINE
Connected to the Internet.

PROTOCOL
A set of rules that determine how computers communicate with each other.

SEARCH ENGINE
Site on the WWW where you can search for other Websites.

SERVICE PROVIDER
See Internet Service Provider.

TCP/IP (TRANSMISSION CONTROL PROTOCOL/ INTERNET PROTOCOL)
The protocol used by Internet computers to communicate.

URL (UNIVERSAL RESOURCE LOCATOR)
An address on the Internet. You type a URL into your browser to visit a website.

WEB BROWSER
Software used to view websites. Internet Explorer and Netscape Navigator are two browsers.

WEB PAGE
A single page on a website that can contain text, images, sound, video, and other elements.

WEB SERVER
A computer with a high-speed connection to the Internet that "serves up" Web pages.

WEBSITE
A collection of Web pages that are linked together in a "web."

WORLD WIDE WEB
The term used to refer to all the websites on the Internet that are linked together to form a global "web" of information.

INDEX

ACKNOWLEDGMENTS

PUBLISHER'S ACKNOWLEDGMENTS
Dorling Kindersley would like to thank the following:
Paul Mattock of APM, Brighton, for commissioned photography.
Microsoft Corporation for permission to reproduce screens
from within Microsoft® Internet Explorer.
stadirect.com, altavista.com (AltaVista and the AltaVista logo are
trademarks of AltaVista Company), bbc.co.uk, benjerry.com,
club-europe.co.uk, CNN.com, demon.net, eidos.co.uk, excite.com,
hotbot.com, nfl.com, northernlight.com, winba.com, yahoo!

Every effort has been made to trace the copyright holders.
*The publisher apologizes for any unintentional omissions and would be pleased,
in such cases, to place an acknowledgment in future editions of this book.*